50
KEYSTONE
FAUNA SPECIES
OF THE
PACIFIC NORTHWEST

A POCKET GUIDE

——— ▪ ▪ ———

Collin Varner

UNIVERSITY OF WASHINGTON PRESS

SEATTLE

University of Washington Press
uwapress.uw.edu

Published simultaneously in Canada by Heritage House Publishing Ltd.
heritagehouse.ca

Cataloguing information available from the Library of Congress

ISBN 9780295752891

Edited by Warren Layberry
Cover and interior book design by Rafael Chimicatti
Cover photographs, clockwise from top left: Peregrine falcon by I Am birdsaspoetry.com (Flickr/CC BY 2.0); yellowjacket wasp by nechaev-kon/iStockphoto; Anna's hummingbird by USFWS Pacific Southwest Region (Flickr/CC BY 2.0); chinook salmon by CoreyFord/iStockphoto; cougar by GlobalP/iStockphoto; red sea urchin by DPFishCo/iStockphoto; bighorn sheep by mdesigner125/iStockphoto; and showshoe hare by impr2003/iStockphoto.
Interior photographs by Collin Varner unless otherwise indicated.
Map by Eric Leinberger

The interior of this book was produced on FSC®-certified, acid-free paper, processed chlorine free and printed with vegetable-based inks.

28 27 26 25 24   1 2 3 4 5

Printed in China

CONTENTS

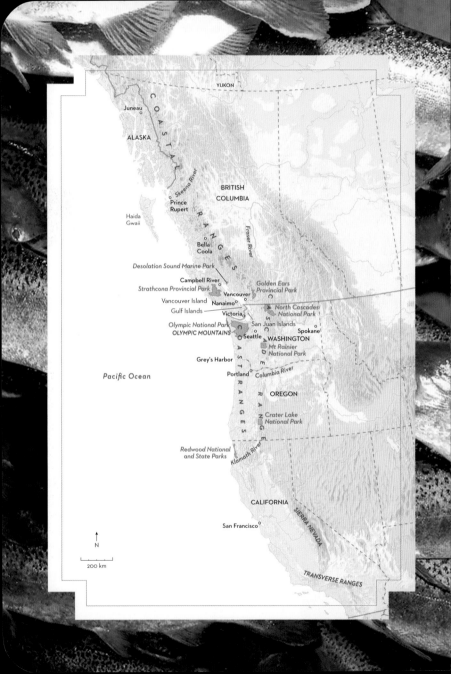

INTERCONNECTEDNESS WITH NATURE

WITHIN COAST SALISH CULTURE, specifically in the Squamish language, Skwxwú7mesh sníchim, we have a word "nchú7mut," which we translate to "one heart, one mind." Coast Salish Peoples have a worldview that includes all beings and walks of life living in harmony with one another. Rather than seeing each species as an individual and standalone anima, we have always seen the gifts and roles that each living organism plays. Many of our languages have names that are related to the sounds that the animals make, or relationships that the animals have to the ecosystem around them.

When looking at the keystone species, as explained through this book, it's important to see the way that each of these animals in the Pacific Northwest are part of a natural community or ecosystem. While you learn more about these keystone species, take a moment to see what they see and to learn about the relationships they have with nature; consider what other animals, plants, waterways these species rely on to survive. As well, acknowledge the effect of seasonal changes and take time every season to reflect on the animals' relationships with the changing environment. Think about how human activity can have an impact on the livelihood and well being of these keystone species. What can you do to give back to the forests, trails, waterways, and natural areas in both urban and wilderness spaces where you can continue to observe these beautiful animals and help them thrive?

Senákw, Senaqwila Wyss
Skwxwú7mesh Ethnobotanist

INTRODUCTION

THIS BOOK PRESENTS fifty keystone species of fauna, some common some less common and all native to coastal British Columbia and the Pacific Northwest. It is not exhaustive by any means and is meant purely as a survey of some important species and aspires to illustrate the roles they play in the ecosystem of the PNW. The choice of animals in this book was a difficult one as the hundreds of different species of terrestrial and marine fauna in the PNW all play important roles in maintaining a healthy ecosystem. The species discussed in this book are a small sample of what the keen observer can discover in our forests and seaside.

A broader, more in-depth approach to the fauna of the region can be found in *The Flora and Fauna of Coastal British Columbia and the Pacific Northwest* (2021) to which this book can be seen as a companion of sorts. A second book presenting fifty keystone flora species of the PNW is also available.

The species in this book have been sorted into five categories, namely, amphibians, birds, fish and marine invertebrates, insects and land invertebrates, and mammals. **The species in each section have been listed alphabetically under broader categories based on their families or sub-families, such as corvids, salmon, or bears, which are noted on the left edge of each species profile**. An index beginning on page 122 lists not only primary common names, but the alternative common names associated with each species.

Most of the photographs in this book were taken by myself as I explored the coastal region over a period of several years. Written with the average observer in mind, the book has an intentional bias towards fauna that are visible to the typical viewer rather than more obscure species. However, it is also a designed to be a quick, useful resource for readers of all levels of expertise.

For the purposes of this book, the Pacific Northwest (PNW) is defined as the region stretching from Juneau, Alaska, to San Francisco, California, from the mainland coast to approximately 100 kilometres (60 miles) inland, as well as the various coastal islands.

Despite the Pacific Northwest being a very large and diverse region, the species within it are relatively uniform. Yet, venture another 50 kilometres (30 miles) inland and the ecosystem is vastly different. The species covered by this book are the delights that the ambler encounters, from the intertidal to the subalpine areas.

What is a Keystone Species?

The topmost stone in an arch is known as the keystone; it is the last stone set in place by the mason, and if it is removed, the entire arch collapses. Like an arch supported by the carefully counterbalanced forces of its stones, an ecosystem is supported by the complex interaction of the species comprising it. The loss of one species will often ripple across an entire ecosystem, sometimes with unforeseen consequences.

In the PNW, perhaps no better illustration of the importance of keystone species exists than that of the sea otter (*Enhydra lutris*). The fur of the sea otter is the densest of any mammal on Earth; it is thick, warm, and naturally waterproof, and starting in the late eighteenth century it nearly doomed the species into extinction. So highly prized was the fur of the sea otter that, over the course of 160 years, *E. lutris* was all but extirpated through hunting, its population dropping to a perilous one or two thousand individuals from a peak population perhaps as high as 300,000.

The decline of the sea otter population meant a corresponding boom in the sea urchin population, for sea otters were a key urchin predator. The unchecked urchin population proceeded to lay to waste vast sections of kelp forests. Without kelp forests, thousands of species of invertebrates, mammals, fish, and birds lost a food source, shelter, and habitat. This left the entire food chain and ecosystem in disarray. Kelp forests absorb carbon dioxide from seawater and the atmosphere. They also help buffer waves, preventing coastal erosion, and help keep pollutants from reaching the shore. Only a worldwide ban on the hunting of sea otters plus extensive conservation and reintroduction efforts have brought the sea otter population back from the brink.

It is also worth understanding that a keystone is shaped to complete a *specific* arch in the same way that a key is cut to a specific lock. Ecologically speaking, a keystone species evolved in one ecosystem will rarely fulfill the same role if introduced into another. Nature does not work that way. European rabbits in Britain are considered a keystone species. They are a good source of food and beneficial in ground disturbing by burrowing warrens, grazing, and recycling nutrients in their scat. In the 1850s, Australia introduced European rabbits into their landscape to be hunted for sport. With no natural predators, the rabbit population exploded to over 600 million by 1940. Even with using biological controls, it is estimated Australia still has 200 million feral rabbits. Their entire ecosystem has been altered for the worse.

The final and perhaps most important takeaway from the keystone analogy, however, is this: While it's true that the removal of the keystone means the collapse of the arch, the larger truth is that the removal of any stone from an arch will compromise its integrity leaving it more susceptible to collapse. The same is true for an ecosystem, the architecture of which represents a profoundly complex dance of evolution and adaptation and from which the removal of any species represents a potential threat to the whole.

AMPHIBIANS

PACIFIC TREE FROG
Pseudacris regilla

TREE FROG FAMILY Hylidae

ECOLOGICAL ROLE Pacific tree frogs are good environmental indicators. When their populations are low, there is something unbalanced in the ecosystem, whether pollution, habitat loss, or the introduction of bull frogs. The frogs, along with their eggs and tadpoles, are an integral part of the food chain for amphibians, garter snakes, fish, herons, river otters, and the introduced voracious bull frog.

DESCRIPTION The Pacific tree frog is to 5 cm (2 in.) long. It ranges in colour from bright green, to dark green, to brownish, with a black face mask. Some have black blotches on their bodies and heads as well.

ETYMOLOGY The genus name *Pseudacris* means "false locust," while the species name *regilla* means "regal." The sound this frog makes is like a locust's.

HABITAT Shallow marshes and ponds. The Pacific tree frog is the most common frog in the Pacific Northwest. It can be found from BC to California.

BIRDS

AMERICAN CROW
Corvus brachyrhynchos

CROW FAMILY Corvidae

ECOLOGICAL ROLE Crows, like ravens, are omnivorous. They eat seeds and nuts such as acorns and prey on smaller species, mostly invertebrates, but also on animals as large as mice, frogs, and the fledglings of other birds when opportunities present themselves. They too will feed on carrion and will scavenge human garbage, helping to stop diseases.

DESCRIPTION The American crow has a wingspan to 100 cm (39.4 in.), slightly larger than the northwestern crow (*C. caurinus*). It has a length to 50 cm (20 in.), of which almost half is tail. Its plumage is a solid iridescent black similar to other all-black corvids.

ETYMOLOGY The species name *brachyrhynchos* is from the Greek *brachy* [short] and *rhynchus* [bill].

HABITAT American crows can be seen in towns, cities, farmland, beaches, parkland, and open forests. They are mainly absent from thick temperate rainforests. Like the northwestern crow, they gather by the thousands to roost at night.

There are two closely related species of crows native to the PNW: the northwestern crow (*C. caurinus*), which is endemic to the area, and the American crow, which is found across North America.

COMMON RAVEN
Corvus corax

CROW FAMILY Corvidae

ECOLOGICAL ROLE Corvids are a noisy, gregarious group. Omnivorous and intelligent, ravens prey on a wide variety of species and are opportunistic eaters of carrion. They cache food, including seeds and nuts, when they have a surplus. This action helps disperse seeds across the landscape.

DESCRIPTION The common raven is an intelligent bird that is central to west coast Indigenous storytelling. It has a wingspan to 1.4 m (4.6 ft.) and a length to 69 cm (27 in.). The adult raven is completely black; in certain light it seems to have an iridescent purple sheen.

ETYMOLOGY The scientific name *Corvus corax* literally means "crow of crows."

HABITAT Very widespread; found from the Aleutian Islands to California.

STELLER'S JAY
Mountain Jay / Pine Jay
Cyanocitta stelleri

CROW FAMILY Corvidae

ECOLOGICAL ROLE Like fellow corvids, the Steller's jay is an omnivore with a diet that is two parts seeds, nuts, and berries to one part prey—mostly, but not entirely, invertebrates. When presented with a surplus they will cache food which is not always recovered and thus sometimes will germinate.

DESCRIPTION Steller's jay is the provincial bird of British Columbia. It has a wingspan to 48 cm (19 in.) and a length to 30 cm (12 in.). The crested head, neck, and upper back are black; with the exception of the black-barred wing tips, all other plumage is blue.

ETYMOLOGY The genus name *Cyanocitta* is from the Greek *kuands* [dark blue] and *kitta* [jay]. The species name *stelleri* commemorates German naturalist Georg Wilhelm Steller (1709–1746).

HABITAT During mating season, Steller's jays are mainly seen in elevated coniferous forests. In autumn, they move to lower elevations, including urban areas.

There are five jays native to the PNW, including the California scrub-jay (*A. californica*), grey jay (*P. canadensis*), and Steller's jay.

MALLARD
Anas platyrhynchos

DUCK FAMILY Anatidae

ECOLOGICAL ROLE Mallards and their eggs and young are a keystone prey throughout North America, being an important food source for a wide array of predators, including: owls, hawks, and eagles; weasels, racoons, felids, and canids; reptiles; and large predatory fish. They also transport seeds, cuttings, and sometimes small invertebrates from one body of water to another, promoting a wholesome ecosystem.

DESCRIPTION Mallards are the most widespread ducks in the northern hemisphere, being found almost anywhere there is shallow water and vegetation. They have a wingspan to 93 cm (37 in.) and a length to 71 cm (28 in.). The males have an iridescent green head, a bright yellow bill, a narrow white collar, a brown chest with lighter sides, blue exposed wing patches, and black curls above a white tail. The females have an orange bill with a black patch and mottled brown plumage. Both have bright orange feet. Dabbling ducks like the mallard up-end themselves on the water to feed rather than fully submerging as diving ducks do.

ETYMOLOGY The species name *platyrhynchos* is from the Greek *platurhunkhos* [broad billed].

Dabbling ducks are species which up-end themselves on the surface of the water to browse the shallows. These include, among others, the American wigeon (*M. americana*), northern pintail (*A. acuta*), green-winged teal (*A. crecca*), and the mallard.

BUFFLEHEAD
Bucephala albeola

DUCK FAMILY Anatidae

ECOLOGICAL ROLE Like all ducks, buffleheads will sometimes inadvertently disperse seeds, cuttings, and even small invertebrates from one body of water to another, and in so doing help ensure robust ecosystems. Their meat and eggs are food to thousands of species of mammals, birds, fish, reptiles, and amphibians. The duck family are considered the rabbits of the waterfowl world.

DESCRIPTION The bufflehead is the smallest diving duck in North America. It has a wingspan to 61 cm (24 in.) and a length to 40 cm (16 in.). The male has a large, white, triangular patch behind its eyes, an iridescent dark green–purple head, a black back, and white underparts. The female has an oval white cheek patch and is dark overall with paler underparts.

ETYMOLOGY The species name *albeola* means "white." The common name bufflehead is a hybrid of buffalo and head. The buffalo look is most noticeable when the male puffs out its head feathers.

HABITAT Breeds in lakes and ponds in Alaska and across northern Canada. Spends the winter along the Pacific coast.

Diving ducks are species which submerge themselves entirely in order to feed. These include, among others, the common goldeneye (*B. clangula*), the harlequin duck (*H. histrionicus*), the surf scoter (*M. perspicillata*), and the bufflehead.

BAND-TAILED PIGEON
Columba fasciata

PIGEON FAMILY Columbidae

ECOLOGICAL ROLE The band-tailed pigeon provides an important food source for raptors, while its eggs are a natural draw for crows, ravens, jays, squirrels, and raccoons.

DESCRIPTION The band-tailed pigeon is the largest pigeon in North America. It has a wingspan to 66 cm (26 in.) and a length to 38 cm (15 in.). The overall plumage is blue-grey with a white bar on the back of the neck and a pale grey band on the tail. The beak is yellow with a black tip.

ETYMOLOGY The genus name *Columba* means "pigeon" or "dove." The species name *fasciata* means "banded" or "striped."

HABITAT Breeds in coniferous forests in the Pacific Northwest. Its favourite foods are arbutus berries, cascara, holly, and Garry oak acorns.

MOURNING DOVE
Zenaida macroura

DOVE FAMILY Columbidae

ECOLOGICAL ROLE The mourning dove provides a food source for hawks and falcons, while their eggs and young attract crows, ravens, jays, squirrels, and raccoons.

DESCRIPTION The mourning dove has a length to 30 cm (12 in.) and a wingspan to 43 cm (17 in.). The overall plumage is greyish brown, with lighter underparts, dark spots on the wings, and one spot on each side of the neck.

ETYMOLOGY The mourning dove is so named because of its call. The genus name *Zenaida* commemorates Princess Zénaïde (1801–1854), the wife of Charles Lucien Bonaparte.

HABITAT Found in a wide variety of areas, including fields, open forests, parks, and near bird feeders, from central BC to Mexico.

BALD EAGLE
Haliaeetus leucocephalus

HAWK FAMILY Accipitridae

ECOLOGICAL ROLE Both the bald eagle and golden eagle (*A. chrysaetos*) are important apex predators, but both will resort to eating carrion if prey is scarce. Bald eagles prey primarily on fish and will end up dispersing partially eaten salmon carcasses on the forest floor, which helps fertilize the soil.

DESCRIPTION The bald eagle has a length of up to 1 m (3.3 ft.) and a wingspan to 2 m (6.6 ft.). It can weigh up to 6.5 kg (14 lb.). It takes five years to get its snow-white head, neck, and tail. Bald eagles are known to wait patiently in high trees observing ospreys diving for fish. When the osprey finally catches a fish, the eagle will swoop down and steal the catch.

ETYMOLOGY The scientific name *Haliaeetus leucocephalus* means "sea eagle with white head." The common name bald comes from "piebald," meaning "contrasting colours" or "black and white."

There are two species of eagles in the Pacific Northwest, the golden eagle (*A. chrysaetos*) and the bald eagle. The latter is endemic to North America while the former is the most broadly distributed eagle in the world. Both are keystone species.

OSPREY
Pandion haliaetus

FALCON FAMILY Falconidae

ECOLOGICAL ROLE Ospreys are reliable indicators of the health of our waterways, both fresh and salt. They are specialists in catching fish and very rarely eat small reptiles, mammals, or birds. Ospreys consume approximately 300 g of fish per catch, so if the fish weighs 400 g, the remaining 100 g is discarded. This excess meat either feeds smaller birds or mammals or is decomposed to enrich the surrounding soil.

DESCRIPTION It weighs 1.4–2 kg (3–4.4 lb.), has a wingspan to 180 cm (71 in.), and can be up to 61 cm (24 in.) in length. The upper plumage is dark brown, with white undersides. The head is mostly white, with a brown line to the eye.

ETYMOLOGY The osprey is called "fish eagle" in many countries because its diet is almost exclusively fish. The genus name *Pandion* is an homage to the mythical Greek king with the same name, while the species name *haliaetus* means "sea eagle."

HABITAT Almost anywhere there are water and fish. It has a worldwide distribution in all continents except Antarctica.

PEREGRINE FALCON
Falco peregrinus

FALCON FAMILY Falconidae

ECOLOGICAL ROLE Peregrine falcons are aerial hunters; they strike their prey in flight at amazing speeds. Traditionally their nesting sites were on cliffs, but with the encroachment of cities, they have adapted to bridges and high rises. Their city diet is primarily made up of pigeons and songbirds.

DESCRIPTION The peregrine falcon is the fastest-diving bird in the world, with speeds up to 320 kph (200 mph.). It has a length to 50 cm (20 in.) and a wingspan to 1.1 m (3.6 ft.). The head is dark with a yellow eye ring and a dark moustache. It has a bluish-grey back and white underparts with dark barring and spots.

ETYMOLOGY The genus name *Falco* means "curved blade," referring to the hooked beak, while the species name *peregrinus* means "travelling" or "wandering," referring to the huge areas it can cover.

There are six species of falcon native to the PNW, including the gyrfalcon (*F. rusticolus*), the merlin (*F. columbarius*), and the peregrine falcon.

COOPER'S HAWK
Accipiter cooperii

■

HAWK FAMILY Accipitridae

ECOLOGICAL ROLE Hawks are keen eyed predators whose main diet comprises mice, squirrels, ground squirrels, rabbits, and voles. Hawks have eyesight eight times better than humans and can spot a mouse from 33 metres (100 ft.).

DESCRIPTION Cooper's hawk is a crow-sized raptor 375–700 g (13–25 oz.) in weight, with a wingspan of 62–94 cm (24–37 in.) and a length of 38–48 cm (15–19 in.). The male is smaller than the female. Mature Cooper's hawks have a dark cap, red eyes, blue-grey upper plumage, and light underparts with reddish-brown bars.

ETYMOLOGY Cooper's hawk was named by French naturalist Charles Lucien Bonaparte, the nephew of French emperor Napoleon Bonaparte, in 1828. The species name *cooperii* commemorates William Cooper (1798–1864), an American zoologist and naturalist.

HABITAT Prefers coniferous or deciduous forests for breeding and hunting. Ranges from southern Canada to northern Mexico but winters as far away as Central America.

There are ten species of hawk native to the PNW, including the red-tailed hawk (*B. jamaicensis*), the northern harrier (*C. hudsonius*), and the Cooper's hawk.

ANNA'S HUMMINGBIRD
Calypte anna

HUMMINGBIRD FAMILY Trochilidae

ECOLOGICAL ROLE Like most hummingbirds, *C. anna* feeds on nectar. In doing this, their beaks and faces get covered in pollen. A lot of trumpet-shaped flowers, such as columbines and honeysuckles, are thought to have evolved for these key pollinators because bees, wasps, moths, and other birds cannot easily access the long tubes. Hummingbirds not only pollinate, but they also eat mosquitoes and aphids.

DESCRIPTION Anna's hummingbird has a wingspan to 13 cm (5 in.) and a length to 10 cm (4 in.). Both the male and the female have iridescent green upperparts. The male has a dark rose-red crown, neck, and throat and greyish underparts. The female has a spotted throat and greyish-white underparts.

ETYMOLOGY The genus name *Calypte* is from the Greek *kaluptre* [a woman's veil], referring to the shining hoods of the male hummingbirds. The species name *anna* commemorates Anne Debelle (1802–1887), Princess of Essling and wife of collector François Victor Masséna, Prince of Essling.

HABITAT Woodlands, parks, and gardens. Some Anna's hummingbirds are permanent residents of the Pacific Northwest.

GREAT HORNED OWL
Bubo virginianus

TRUE OWL FAMILY Strigidae

ECOLOGICAL ROLE With their incredible vision, acute hearing, sharp beaks, strong talons, specially adapted feathers that allow them to fly in absolute silence, and heads that turn 270 degrees, great horned owls are apex predators of the night.

DESCRIPTION Great horned owls are the most widely dispersed owls in North and South America. They can weigh up to 2.5 kg (5.5 lb.) and have a wingspan up to 1.5 m (5 ft.) and a length of 46–64 cm (18–25 in.). The upper plumage is a mottled grey-brown, with thin horizontal barring below. The top of the head is flat with large ear tufts on the sides.

ETYMOLOGY The species name *virginianus* is from the Virginia colonies of eastern North America, which were named for the Virgin Queen, Queen Elizabeth I of England (1533–1603).

HABITAT With the amount of area great horned owls cover, they have adapted well to and can be found in extremely diverse habitats, including forests, deserts, shorelines, and marshes. They range from Alaska to the tip of South America, from the east coast to the west coast.

There are more than a dozen species of owl in the PNW ranging in size from the diminutive saw-whet owl (*A. acadicus*) to the great horned owl.

TRUMPETER SWAN
Cygnus buccinator

DUCK FAMILY Anatidae

ECOLOGICAL ROLE The size of adult trumpeter swans makes them all but immune to predation, but their eggs and cygnets provide a food source to all manner of predators. Their dabbling for food helps ensure that river, lake, and pond bottoms are turned over and kept renewed.

DESCRIPTION Trumpeter swans are the largest waterfowl in North America. They have a wingspan to 2.4 m (7.9 ft.) and a length to 1.65 m (5.4 ft.). The overall plumage is snow white, with a straight black bill. Juveniles have grey plumage.

ETYMOLOGY The species name *buccinator* is from the Latin *buccina* [military trumpet].

HABITAT Breeds in Alaska and northern BC. Migrates to the Pacific Northwest between October and November.

TURKEY VULTURE
Cathartes aura

VULTURE FAMILY Cathartidae

ECOLOGICAL ROLE Vultures fulfil an important ecological role by subsisting on carrion and consuming the meat of fish, reptiles, birds, amphibians, insects, and mammals. They prefer fresh meat but consume decayed flesh and have developed a remarkable tolerance to a broad range of pathogens.

DESCRIPTION The turkey vulture is one of North America's largest birds of prey. It can weigh as much as 2.3 kg (5.1 lb.), with a wingspan of up to 183 cm (72 in.) and a length of 62–81 cm (24–32 in.). The overall plumage is brownish-black, with the underwing flight feathers having a silver tinge. The disproportionately small head is red and featherless, with an ivory-coloured beak.

ETYMOLOGY The genus name *Cathartes* means "cleanser" or "purifier."

HABITAT Beaches, forested hillsides, and back roads, looking for roadkill. Turkey vultures are mainly summer dwellers in most of Oregon, Washington, and southern British Columbia. They winter in southern USA into Mexico and Central America.

ACORN WOODPECKER
Melanerpes formicivorus

WOODPECKER FAMILY Picidae

ECOLOGICAL ROLE Woodpeckers are effectively the master carpenters of the avian world. They excavate holes in trees for their nests and only use them for one breeding season. In the following years, the abandoned holes become home to countless species of birds and mammals, such as saw-whet owls, screech owls, wood ducks, swallows, wrens, grey and flying squirrels, opossums, and mice. In fact, older dead or living trees that have multiple woodpecker holes are valuable real estate and become condominiums of the forest.

DESCRIPTION The acorn woodpecker is aptly named for the way it stores acorns in the bark of trees. It is slightly smaller than an American robin, with a wingspan to 30 cm (12 in.) and a length to 23 cm (9 in.). The male has a yellowish forecrown; the female has a black forecrown. Both have a black neck, black wings, a black tail, white underparts, white wing patches, and a white rump.

ETYMOLOGY The genus name *Melanerpes* means "tree creeper" or "woodpecker." The species name *formicivorus* means "ant eating."

HABITAT Common in Oregon and California, where there are oak trees. The acorn woodpecker gathers acorns in the autumn and stores them in snug holes for later consumption. Because of their soft bark, pines and Douglas firs are mainly used as storage trees.

There are eleven species of woodpeckers in the PNW including the hairy and downy woodpeckers (*D. villosus* and *D. pubescens*), the pileated woodpecker (*D. pileatus*), the northern flicker (*C. auratus*), and the acorn woodpecker

FISH & MARINE INVERTEBRATES

DUNGENESS CRAB
Metacarcinus magister

CRAB FAMILY Cancridae

ECOLOGICAL ROLE Dungeness crabs are opportunistic predators, feeding on bivalves, shrimp, small live fish, and almost any animal carcasses. They are considered marine decomposers and janitors by cleaning up ocean floors through the harvesting of dead plant and animal matter. The crabs themselves, in all stages of their life cycle, are prey to sea otters, wolf eels, Pacific octopuses, and Pacific halibut.

DESCRIPTION The Dungeness crab is to 25 cm (10 in.) across. The carapace (shell) varies in colour from grey-brown to red-brown-purple. The claws are yellow orange with white tips.

ETYMOLOGY The common name is derived from Dungeness Bay in Washington State.

HABITAT On sandy-bottomed areas from Alaska to California.

There are dozens of species of crab native to the PNW, including green and purple shore crabs (*H. oregonensis* and *H. nudus*), red rock crab (*C. productus*), and Dungeness crab.

GIANT PACIFIC OCTOPUS
Enteroctopus dofleini

OCTOPUS FAMILY Octopodidae

ECOLOGICAL ROLE Giant Pacific octopuses are more predators than prey. Their diet is mainly small fish, clams, crabs, shrimp, and scallops. A 124 kg (300 lb.) octopus will eat about 5 kg (12 lb.) of food per day. They are a food source for sea lions, harbour seals, sea otters, and sharks. The young octopuses are food for wolf eels and halibut.

DESCRIPTION The giant Pacific octopus is to 9 m (30 ft.) across but is more typically seen at 2 m (6.6 ft.). The body and eight legs are red to brown, depending on the colour of its habitat. It is the largest octopus in the world.

ETYMOLOGY The genus name *Enteroctopus* means "giant octopus," while the species name *dofleini* commemorates German zoologist Franz Theodor Doflein (1873–1924).

HABITAT Along the coast from Alaska to California, sometimes in tide pools. The photo on the facing page is of a captive octopus named Fred at the Sidney Aquarium on Vancouver Island.

CHINOOK SALMON
Spring Salmon
Oncorhynchus tshawytscha

SALMON FAMILY Salmonidae

ECOLOGICAL ROLE Pacific salmon species are one of the most bene-ficial animals on earth. They feed the world when alive and also when they die. When in the ocean, Pacific salmon are the main food source for the southern resident orcas—without salmon, their existence is crit-ically jeopardized. Harbour seals and sea lions also depend on Pacific salmon. When migrating in the rivers, streams, and estuaries, their ex-hausted bodies feed black bears, grizzlies, wolves, eagles, gulls, crows, river otters, and ravens. The trees and plants along the inland migration routes greatly benefit from the nutrition from the decomposing carcasses.

DESCRIPTION The chinook salmon, also known as the spring salmon, is 61–91 cm (24–36 in.) long and 9–23 kg (20–50 lb.). Longer and heavier specimens have also been recorded. It is blue green on the back, with silver sides and a spotted tail.

ETYMOLOGY The species name *tshawytscha* is Greek for "hood nose," referring to the hooked jaws of the males in mating season.

HABITAT Ocean and coastal rivers from Alaska to California.

Pacific salmon species include coho (*O. kisutch*), chum (*O. keta*), sockeye (*O. nerka*), pink salmon (*O. gorbuscha*), and chinook.

PURPLE SEA URCHIN
Strongylocentrotus purpuratus

SEA URCHIN FAMILY Strongylocentrotidae

ECOLOGICAL ROLE Purple sea urchins are omnivores that feed primarily on kelp and algae, but they also scavenge fallen animal matter. Though they can and have devoured kelp forests, if they can be kept in balance, they are an integral link in the marine ecosystem chain.

CONSERVATION STATUS Near Threatened.

DESCRIPTION The purple sea urchin is to 10 cm (4 in.) across. The shell and spines are purple-pinkish to greenish.

ETYMOLOGY The genus name *Strongylocentrotus* means "ball of spines."

HABITAT Rocky shorelines from Alaska to California.

GIANT PINK STAR
Pisaster brevispinus

SEA STAR FAMILY Asteriidae

ECOLOGICAL ROLE Giant pink stars are carnivorous scavengers cleaning the ocean floor of carrion. Their main diet is bivalves like clams, cockles, and mussels, but they also consume sand dollars. They are a food source for sea otters and other species of stars. Gulls will attempt to make a meal of them at low tide.

DESCRIPTION The giant pink star is to 60 cm (2 ft.) across. It has five bristly arms and is pink to whitish grey. The size of this star allows it to catch bigger prey, including clams, sand dollars, and giant barnacles.

ETYMOLOGY The species name *brevispinus* refers to another common name of this star, short-spined star.

HABITAT Areas with sandy mud where there are clams. Found from Alaska to California.

INSECTS & LAND INVERTEBRATES

MIXED BUMBLEBEE
Fuzzy-Horned Bumblebee
Bombus mixtus

BUMBLEBEE AND HONEYBEE FAMILY Apidae

ECOLOGICAL ROLE The importance of bees as pollinators cannot be overstated. Bumblebees have a unique method of dislodging hard-to-get-at pollen, referred to as buzz pollination. The bee grasps the flower in its mouth and buzzes her wings, which will unseat the pollen. Bumblebees can also forage in lower temperatures and with less light than most other bees. This gives them the advantage of longer pollination days and a broader range of elevations at which they can pollinate.

DESCRIPTION The mixed bumblebee is to 1.3 cm (0.5 in.) long. The head and body are covered in yellow and black hairs. The tip of the abdomen is red brown.

ETYMOLOGY The species name *mixtus* refers to the mixed colours.

HABITAT The mixed bumblebee is a west coast species that feeds on nectar.

There are hundreds of species of bees found in the PNW, including 38 species of bumblebees.

PACIFIC BANANA SLUG
Leopard Banana Slug
Ariolimax columbianus

ROUND BACK SLUG FAMILY Arionidae

ECOLOGICAL ROLE Banana slugs are detritivores: they feed on dead plant material, animal feces, mushrooms, animal carcasses, and fallen leaves. Their excrement is nitrogen rich, which makes an excellent fertilizer and soil humus. Also, their excrement can contain seeds and spores which can be slowly transported several metres making the slugs important to the forest ecosystem. Banana slugs are prey to salamanders, garter snakes, raccoons, millipedes, porcupines, crows, ducks, geese, beetles, and newts. Raccoons can be seen rolling young slugs in dry sand or soil which absorbs the slime. If eaten directly, the slime will numb their tongues.

DESCRIPTION The Pacific banana slug grows to 25 cm (10 in.) in length. Its colours can range from bright yellow (which gives it the common name of banana slug), to greenish, to brown, to black and brown (which gives it another common name, leopard banana slug), to white. Colours vary with age, diet, moisture, and light. The Pacific banana slug is the second-largest slug in the world. The slimy excretion that banana slugs produce serves multiple purposes: it helps with respiration, attracts mates, and aids in locomotion.

HABITAT Common in moist Pacific Northwest forests and gardens.

CROSS ORBWEAVER
Diadem Spider
Araneus diadematus

ORB-WEAVER FAMILY Araneidae

ECOLOGICAL ROLE Orbweaver spiders are generalist insect predators, eating almost anything that flies or crawls into their web, including mosquitoes, flies, wasps, bees, moths, and beetles. Interestingly they eat their own webs on a regular basis, digesting any air borne pollen or fungal spores caught in the strands, which makes them omnivores not pure carnivores.

DESCRIPTION The male cross orbweaver's body is to 0.7 cm (0.3 in.) across, and the female's is to 1.5 cm (0.6 in.) across. The colouration is red to brown, with a series of white dots that form a cross. Variations of colours and patterns can be found in different regions.

ETYMOLOGY The genus name *Aranaeus* is from the Latin *arane* [spider].

HABITAT Most often seen at the end of summer and in autumn, spinning their orb-like webs.

The PNW boasts more than 500 species of spiders, including the giant house spider (*E. duellica*), goldenrod crab spider (*M. vatia*), western black widow (*L. Hesperus*), and cross orbweaver.

PACIFIC DAMPWOOD TERMITE
Zootermopsis angusticollis

DAMPWOOD TERMITE FAMILY Termopsidae

ECOLOGICAL ROLE Dampwood termites perform an ecological service by decomposing moist dead wood, returning the nutrients and other organic matter to the forest soil. Termites also tunnel, which in turn, aerates and improves the soil structure.

DESCRIPTION The Pacific dampwood termite has a length to 2.5 cm (1 in.). Nymphs have a white body and a red head. Soldiers are reddish orange-brown, with pincers on their heads. The Pacific dampwood termite is one of the largest termites in North America.

ETYMOLOGY The species name *angusticollis* is from the Latin *angustus* [narrow] and *collum* [neck].

HABITAT Usually seen in forests with rotting stumps and logs. Flying termites are females looking for a mate.

WESTERN YELLOWJACKET
Vespula pensylvanica

WASP FAMILY Vespidae

ECOLOGICAL ROLE As annoying as yellowjackets can be, they are key predators and the PNW would be overrun with spiders and insects without them. The voracious appetite of their young helps keep the spider and insect world in check. Adult wasps feed on sugar from nectar and aphids as well as man-made sugars. They also play a role in the consumption of carrion. The insects they capture—spiders, caterpillars, crickets, and beetles—are fed to their young. In one season, adult wasps capture millions of insects in the PNW.

DESCRIPTION The western yellowjacket grows to 2.5 cm (1 in.). They are yellow and black, with alternating bands on the abdomen. Yellowjackets have a barbed, lance-like stinger that can sting repeatedly.

HABITAT Very common in forests and urban areas in the Pacific Northwest. Their nests can be found in trees and rodent burrows.

There are half a dozen species of ground yellowjacket in the PNW including the Alaska yellowjacket (*V. alascensis*), the blackjacket (*V. consobrina*), and the western yellowjacket.

MAMMALS

AMERICAN BADGER
Taxidea taxus

WEASEL FAMILY Mustelidae

ECOLOGICAL ROLE The elusive American badgers play a key role in the PNW grasslands. Their powerful front legs with long claws dig tunnels and burrows for their own dwellings, but also to pursue ground squirrels, voles, mice, reptiles, and insects. The large amounts of subterranean soils they excavate mix with the top layer compost and other soils, improving aeration and surrounding soils.

DESCRIPTION Male American badgers can weigh up to 15 kg (33 lb.) while healthy females can weigh up to 9.5 kg (21 lb.). Males are slightly larger than females, averaging 60–75 cm (23.5–29.5 in.) in length. Their body fur is a combination of brown and black with grizzled tips, giving them a greying appearance. Their masked faces are black and white with a white stripe running from the nose to the back of the head.

ETYMOLOGY The common name badger is from the white and black marks on their faces (badges). In more recent times, the term "to badger someone" means "to harass or annoy," presumably taken from the badger's aggressive disposition.

HABITAT Badgers usually use abandoned burrows to make their dens, which will have several tunnels and separate chambers. They are mainly an inland mammal, but they do appear on the Pacific coast in Oregon, California, and Mexico.

LITTLE BROWN BAT
Myotis lucifugus

EVENING BAT FAMILY Vespertilionidae

ECOLOGICAL ROLE Little brown bats are insectivores and the perfect mosquito-eating machines. They are one of the best natural methods of controlling outbreaks of flying insects. Without them, the PNW would be inundated with moths, their leaf-eating offspring, flying beetles, and mosquitoes. In a night's foraging, they can consume up to their own body weight in insects (approx. 100 g). Not only are they protecting us from biting mosquitoes, they are reducing the spread of diseases for which mosquitoes can serve as vectors.

CONSERVATION STATUS Endangered

DESCRIPTION Little brown bats have a length to 10 cm (4 in.) and a wingspan to 25 cm (10 in.). The glossy fur on the upperparts is dark brown to golden brown, with the underparts being paler.

ETYMOLOGY The species name *lucifugus* is Latin for "fear of the light" or "shunning of the light."

HABITAT The little brown bat occupies three types of roosts: day, night, and hibernation. The day and night roosts are usually in buildings or trees near water. The hibernation roost is usually in caves or old mines, where the temperature does not fall below freezing. Found from southern Alaska to California.

There are more than a dozen species of bats present in the PNW, including the Townsend's big-eared bat (*C. townsendii*), silver-haired bat (*L. noctivagans*), big brown bat (*E. fuscus*), and little brown bat.

BLACK BEAR
Ursus americanus

BEAR FAMILY Ursidae

ECOLOGICAL ROLE American black bears and grizzly bears are the apex land mammals in the PNW. Neither are obligate predators but rather impressive omnivores. Their massive shoulders and long claws allow them to move logs and boulders in search for insects and small burrowing animals. In doing this, they aerate the soil and usually mix in the compost layer for a more nourishing medium.

DESCRIPTION The black bear is to 1.8 m (5.9 ft.) in length and can stand to 1.1 m (3.6 ft.) at the shoulder. Though it is called the black bear, its colouring can also range in shades from tan to brown. There is also the rare Kermode bear (*U. americanus kermodei*), which is white to creamy white. It is a subspecies of the black bear.

ETYMOLOGY The genus and species names literally translate into American bear.

HABITAT Forested areas, mountains, salmon streams and rivers, and garbage dumps, from Alaska to California.

GRIZZLY BEAR
Ursus arctos

BEAR FAMILY Ursidae

ECOLOGICAL ROLE When grizzlies and black bears hunt for salmon, they will usually carry the caught fish into the forest. The uneaten portions, bones, skin, and flesh, will decompose and fertilize the forest. Before hibernating, a male grizzly can consume as many as 200,000 berries a day, producing a lot of scat. Considering that a solitary bear can walk up to 64 km (40 mi.) a day, there is a lot of area to deposit the berry seeds.

DESCRIPTION The grizzly bear is about 1.4–2.9 m (4.6–9.2 ft.) in length and can have a shoulder height of about 0.7–1.5 m (2.3–4.9 ft.). It can range in colour from tan to brown to almost black. Most of the bears have white tips at the end of their hair, giving them a grizzled look.

ETYMOLOGY The genus name *Ursus* is Latin for "bear," while the species name *arctos* is Greek for "bear."

HABITAT The grizzly bear once ranged across a large portion of North America, including northern Mexico. In the Pacific Northwest, grizzly bears can be seen in coastal BC, especially when the salmon are spawning. They move from higher elevations to lower elevations when the berries are ripening and then move higher again to follow the ripening fruit. Alaska has the largest concentration in North America.

AMERICAN BEAVER
Castor canadensis

BEAVER FAMILY Castoridae

ECOLOGICAL ROLE Beavers are the engineers of North American forests. Their wood and mud dams collect vegetation, sediments, and silts, which are processed into nutrient-rich freshwater wetlands. This, in turn, attracts diverse plant, animal, fish, and waterfowl. The wetlands can also mitigate flooding and droughts.

DESCRIPTION The American beaver has a length from 74–90 cm (29–35 in.) and a weight of 11–32 kg (24–71 lb.). It has dark-brown fur, webbed back feet, orange incisors, and a flat tail from 20–35 cm (8–14 in.) long. The American beaver is the largest rodent in North America; it comes second in the world after the South American capybara. The beaver waterproofs its fur by coating it with castoreum, an oily secretion from its scent glands.

ETYMOLOGY The genus name *Castor* comes from the secretion castoreum.

HABITAT Ponds, streams, rivers, and lakes. Almost anywhere there is fresh water and deciduous trees.

COYOTE
Canis latrans

■

CANID FAMILY Canidae

ECOLOGICAL ROLE The coyote's variable diet of meat, poultry, fruit, berries, grasses, and eggs have made them masters of survival. What wolves don't take down, coyotes will. They are the apex species for regulating the populations of smaller species: raccoons, skunks, rats, mice, squirrels, and birds. These wily predators are critical for keeping a balance in the PNW food chain.

DESCRIPTION The coyote is to 1.4 m (4.6 ft.) in length, with a shoulder height to 60 cm (24 in.). The colour of the fur varies geographically; in the Pacific Northwest, the fur is usually whitish grey with hints of red.

ETYMOLOGY The species name *latrans* means "to bark."

HABITAT Almost anywhere it can find food, including urban areas, parks, forests, and fields. The diet of the coyote is extremely varied, including mice, squirrels, birds, reptiles, and, when in season, berries. Found from southern Alaska to California.

GREY WOLF
Timber Wolf
Canis lupus

CANID FAMILY Canidae

ECOLOGICAL ROLE The ability of grey wolves to organize and hunt in packs has made them apex hunters and a keystone species. They are obligate carnivores—as opposed to coyotes—and prefer large ungulates such as deer, elk, moose, caribou, and bison, but will hunt smaller prey when forced to. This has a top-down effect on the animal food chain, allowing smaller animals to fill in the feeding gaps. As much as cattle ranchers dislike wolves, they are critically important to their prey beneath them and their prey's plant chain beneath them.

DESCRIPTION The grey wolf has a length from 1.4–2 m (4.6–6.6 ft.) and a shoulder height to 1 m (3.3 ft.). The fur colour ranges from nearly white to black, with grizzled grey being the most common. A dark coat usually indicates that the wolf lives in dense forests; a lighter coat is common where there is lots of snow (when it is known as the Arctic wolf).

ETYMOLOGY The species name *lupus* is Latin for wolf.

HABITAT Along shorelines, in or beside dense forests, in the Pacific Northwest.

There is also a unique subspecies of the grey wolf that is endemic to the coastal PNW: the sea wolf (*C. lupus crassodon*). Also known as the Vancouver coastal sea wolf, it is smaller in size and lives a semi-aquatic life with a diet of up to 90 percent ocean fauna. The sea wolf is comfortable swimming between the smaller islands of the Salish Sea, following salmon runs and foraging clam beds, stranded crabs, and the best mussel and barnacle rocks.

CALIFORNIA GROUND SQUIRREL
Otospermophilus beecheyi

SQUIRREL FAMILY Sciuridae

ECOLOGICAL ROLE Ground squirrels are considered top-down and bottom up keystone species. Top-down because they are an important food source for numerous predator species, from rattlesnakes to coyotes to raptors like bald eagles. Bottom-up because they are also excellent excavators, aerating the soil while mixing horizon soils with top soils, compost, and manures.

DESCRIPTION The California ground squirrel is to 30 cm (12 in.) in length, and its bushy tail is to 15 cm (6 in.) long. The squirrel's upperparts are a mottled or spotted grey-brown, and the underparts are a soft greyish-yellow with black fur around the ears.

ETYMOLOGY The species name *beecheyi* commemorates Frederick William Beechey, a 19th-century British explorer and naval officer.

HABITAT Open, well-drained soils; roadsides; highland near beaches, and farms, especially where grain is grown. Quite common at roadside pullovers along the state highways through Oregon and California—the squirrels come out to get treats from the tourists.

The PNW is home to a dozen species of ground squirrel including the Arctic ground squirrel (*U. parryii*), the hoary marmot (*M. caligata*), the Columbian ground squirrel (*U. columbianus*), and the California ground squirrel.

YELLOW-PINE CHIPMUNK
Northwestern Chipmunk
Tamias amoenus

SQUIRREL FAMILY Sciuridae

ECOLOGICAL ROLE Chipmunks and tree squirrels are nature's dispersers of seeds. Some are larder hoarders, stashing all their seeds in one cache, while some are scatter hoarders, relying on hundreds of small caches. Through summer and fall, squirrels and chipmunks bury seeds, nuts, and other precious food supplies in underground caches. Not only does this disperse those nuts and seeds that remain unrecovered, it also aerates and fertilizes the soil. Studies have shown that scatter hoarders fail to recover up to 70 percent of their cached food.

DESCRIPTION The yellow-pine chipmunk has a total length to 24 cm (9.5 in.) and can weigh up to 73 g (2.6 oz.). These cute little rodents have five longitudinal black-and-white stripes on a cinnamon-coloured coat.

ETYMOLOGY The species name *amoenus* means "beautiful" or "lovely," while the genus name *Tamias* is Greek for "dispenser," "treasurer," or "stewart," which is a fabulous name for this little chipmunk's role in dispersing seeds.

HABITAT In the Pacific Northwest, the yellow-pine chipmunk is usually seen at mid to high elevations that have coniferous forests.

There are half a dozen species of chipmunks scurrying around the PNW, including the Townsend's chipmunk (*N. Townsendii*), the least chipmunk (*N. minimus*), and the yellow-pine chipmunk.

BLACK-TAILED DEER
Columbian Black-Tailed Deer
Odocoileus hemionus ssp. columbianus

DEER FAMILY Cervidae

ECOLOGICAL ROLE An important prey for cougars and grey wolves, their carcasses also feed bears, bobcats, raptors, ravens, crows, insects, and finally the soil itself as fertilizer. Deer are grazers and browsers that feed on grasses, sedges, new leaves and shoots on trees and bushes, and fruit and berries. In winter, with snow on the ground, it is tree bark, lichen, fallen leaves, and twigs that make up any shortfall. Deer help keep meadows from being overtaken by larger trees and are top scat producers, which is important as a source of both fertilizer and seed dispersal.

DESCRIPTION The black-tailed deer is a subspecies of the mule deer. It is smaller than the mule deer, at about 145 cm (57 in.) in length and about 90 cm (35 in.) at the shoulder. It is a darker brown than the mule deer, with a white rump patch and a black tail. The fawns are reddish-brown with white spots. The buck sheds his antlers each winter and grows a new set in the spring.

ETYMOLOGY The species name *hemionus* comes from the Greek *hemi* [half] and *onus* [ass or mule].

HABITAT Very common in open forests with undergrowth. Can be seen from the Alaskan Panhandle to California. The city of Victoria, on Vancouver Island, is overrun with black-tailed deer.

There are seven species of deer in the PNW including moose (*A. alces*), elk (*C. canadensis*), and mule deer, which are by far the most populous.

GREY WHALE
Eschrichtius robustus

GREY WHALE FAMILY Eschrichtiidae

ECOLOGICAL ROLE One of the baleen whales, this coastal species feeds by swimming along the ocean floor, turning on their sides, and scooping up huge mouthfuls of mud, filtering it through their baleen. Despite being known as whalebone, the baleen is actually a series of hardened skin plates that act as a filter or sieve to catch crustaceans and tubeworms. The unique method of feeding sends up magnificent plumes of mud filled with crustaceans to the surface of the water, where there are usually hundreds of seabirds (black-legged kitiwakes, thick-billed mures, northern fulmars, and red phalaropes) waiting to feast on the bounty.

DESCRIPTION The grey whale is a baleen whale to 16 m (52 ft.) long. It has dark-grey skin with light-grey and white mottling. It is often seen with barnacles growing on its skin.

ETYMOLOGY The genus name *Eschrichtius* commemorates zoologist Daniel Frederik Eschricht (1798–1863).

HABITAT Can be seen migrating from Alaska to California.

ORCA
Killer Whale
Orcinus orca

OCEANIC DOLPHIN FAMILY Delphinidae

ECOLOGICAL ROLE Orcas are apex marine mammals and live in all oceans of the world, as do sea lions and seals, two of their main diet staples. Without orcas, sea lions, seals, dolphins, sharks, sea otters, sea birds, squid, and other animal populations would rapidly climb. The presence of orcas in the world's oceans definitely balances the marine's ecosystem.

DESCRIPTION Male orcas range from 7 m (23 ft.) to 9 m (30 ft.) long. Females range from 6 m (20 ft.) to 8 m (26 ft.) long. Typically they are black with a white chest, white sides, and white patches behind the eyes. Orcas are more closely related to dolphins than whales.

ETYMOLOGY The orca was originally named *Delphinus orca*, meaning "demon dolphin."

HABITAT Common in coastal waters from Alaska to Oregon.

COUGAR
Mountain Lion / Puma
Puma concolor

CAT FAMILY Felidae

ECOLOGICAL ROLE Cougars are the apex predator in the forests of the PNW. A healthy cougar has a good chance of walking away from an altercation with even two wolves. Their prowess and strength help keep in check an overabundance of elk, deer, mountain sheep, rabbits, and rodents. In areas where cougars have been removed (usually shot or trapped), the landscape soon becomes overrun by grazing herbivores. A cougar's selective or messy eating habits after a large kill leaves a lot of food for smaller carnivores and omnivores such as skunks, bobcats, foxes, eagles, crows, and vultures. The skeletons of such kills often remain intact, picked clean of meat, and over time decompose back into soil.

DESCRIPTION The cougar is 1.5–2 m (4.9–6.6 ft.) in length and has a shoulder height to 80 cm (31 in.). The coat is a uniform tawny yellow to reddish-brown. The throat, chest, and belly are whitish.

ETYMOLOGY The genus name *Puma* comes from the Peruvian Quechua language, where it means "powerful."

HABITAT Other than humans, the cougar has the largest natural distribution of any terrestrial mammal in the western hemisphere. In the Pacific Northwest, the cougar is most likely to be seen wherever there are deer.

BIGHORN SHEEP
Ovis canadensis

UNGULATE FAMILY Bovidae

ECOLOGICAL ROLE As grazers and browsers, bighorn sheep occupy similar ecological niches and fulfil similar roles to mountain goats. They are an important prey for grey wolves, grizzly bears, and cougars, with lambs being especially susceptible to predation.

DESCRIPTION Both the ewes and the rams have beautifully shaped horns, but it is from the males' large horns that they got their common name, bighorn. Males can weigh up to 143 kg (315 lb.) while females can weigh as much as 91 kg (201 lb.). They range in colour from greyish to dark brown. The males' horns can weigh up to 14 kg (30 lb.) which may exceed the total of the rest of their bones.

ETYMOLOGY The genus name *Ovis* is from the Latin *ovicula* meaning "little sheep."

HABITAT It is thought that the bighorns originally crossed over the Bering Land Bridge from Siberia 15,000 years ago. Their range now is southern BC to Mexico, mainly in the Rocky Mountains.

There are two species of sheep native to the PNW, Dall sheep (*O. dalli*) and bighorn sheep.

MOUNTAIN GOAT
Rocky Mountain Goat
Oreamnos americanus

RUMINANT FAMILY Bovidae

ECOLOGICAL ROLE Mountain goats graze high-altitude alpine meadows and surrounding forests. Their diet is mainly grasses, sedges, clover, willow, sage, lichen, and wildflowers. At lower elevations, they keep the taller woody plants from encroaching on meadows, thus forming fire breaks between forests. These grazers spread seeds from alpine meadows to low-level avalanche tracks, keeping a diverse mix of vegetation throughout their range. Though some adult goats are killed by wolves, coyotes, wolverines, cougars, grizzly bears, and even golden eagles, it is primarily their young (kids) that appear in the food chain.

DESCRIPTION Both male (billies) and female (nannies) mountain goats have black horns, beards, and white, woolly double coats. Males are up to 30 percent larger than females, growing to 140 kg (309 lb.). Their feet are well adapted for alpine climbing: cloven hooves that spread apart with inner pads and dewclaws that keep them stable on steep slopes.

ETYMOLOGY The genus name *Oreamnos* is Greek for "mountain lamb."

HABITAT The mountain goat is endemic to North America and is considered an iconic animal in Alaska, British Columbia, and Washington State. Seen throughout the Rocky Mountains and Cascade Range.

BRUSH RABBIT
Sylvilagus bachmani

RABBIT AND HARE FAMILY Leporidae

ECOLOGICAL ROLE Native to the PNW, the brush rabbit is extremely important for keeping a healthy predator–prey balance. When there are a lot of prey, the predator side increases. With a predator increase, the prey population decreases. This teeter-totter effect balances each other.

DESCRIPTION A relatively small rabbit, from 30–37 cm (11–14.5 in.) long, with a grey tail. It has white fur in winter with black-tipped ears.

HABITAT Found from the Columbia River to southern California, living among brambles along open areas; some sub-species are found only in old-growth forests.

SNOWSHOE HARE
Lepus americanus

RABBIT AND HARE FAMILY Leporidae

ECOLOGICAL ROLE The snowshoe hare is important to a number of predators including coyotes, wolves, hawks, eagles, owls, bobcats, and Canada lynx. So important is the snowshoe hare to the Canada lynx that the two populations are linked with a boom in the snowshoe hare population leading to a rise in the lynx population.

DESCRIPTION At 36–52 cm (14–20 in.) long, the snowshoe hare is the smallest of the *Lepus* genus. It is well adapted to snowy terrain, with white winter fur and long back legs and feet (see inset photo).

HABITAT Found from Alaska to Oregon and eastward.

AMERICAN MINK
Mustela vison

WEASEL FAMILY Mustelidae

ECOLOGICAL ROLE Mink are aquatic and terrestrial carnivores that will eat anything they kill: rats, mice, young rabbits, voles, birds, crabs, clams, frogs, and snakes. Their rare combination of being excellent swimmers, terrestrial runners, and tree climbers allows them to catch prey that may not otherwise have many predators, such as muskrats, bird eggs, and young squirrels. Without this natural control, these species could overpopulate within a couple breeding seasons.

DESCRIPTION The American mink is a semi-aquatic omnivore to 70 cm (28 in.) in length. The luxurious fur is dark brown to black. Its anal scent glands secrete a foul odour, which is mainly used to define its territory.

ETYMOLOGY The genus name *Mustela* is Latin for "weasel." The common name mink is from a Swedish word that means "stinky animal."

HABITAT Mostly seen around waterways, ocean, rivers, streams, and ponds hunting for aquatic food. Can be found from Alaska to California.

NORTHERN RIVER OTTER
North American River Otter
Lontra canadensis

WEASEL FAMILY Mustelidae

ECOLOGICAL ROLE Northern river otters are indicators of a healthy watershed. They do not tolerate polluted water, whether fresh or marine. Their main diet in the PNW comprises fish, frogs, bird eggs, bivalves, young red slider turtles, small rodents, and aquatic plants. River otters help maintain a healthy watershed by thinning out invasive and over-productive species, thus maintaining biodiversity.

DESCRIPTION The northern river otter is to 1.3 m (4.3 ft.) long and can weigh up to 14 kg (31 lb.). The water-repellent fur is dark brown on the back and sides, with lighter underparts.

ETYMOLOGY The genus name *Lontra* means "otter."

HABITAT Common along the coast, from Alaska to California. It can also be found inland in streams and lakes.

SEA OTTER
Enhydra lutris

WEASEL FAMILY Mustelidae

ECOLOGICAL ROLE The quintessential example of the importance of a keystone species in the PNW. The fur of the sea otter is the densest of any mammal on Earth; it is thick, warm, naturally waterproof, and thus was highly prized. As a result of hunting for the fur trade, the sea otter population plummeted from about 300,000 to near extinction at about 1,000–2,000 individuals.

The decline of the sea otter population in the 1800s led to cascading devastation across the ocean and intertidal ecosystems along the West Coast. Sea urchins, a key part of sea otter diet, boomed in population and laid waste to swathes of kelp forests. This, in turn, meant that thousands of species of invertebrates, mammals, fish, and birds lost a food source, shelter, and habitat. As well, the loss of kelp forests as a buffer before the shore meant less carbon dioxide sequestering or filtering of ocean pollutants, and greater shoreline erosion. Only a worldwide ban on the hunting of sea otters plus extensive conservation and reintroduction efforts have brought the sea otter population, and its dependent ecosystem, back from the brink.

CONSERVATION STATUS Endangered.

DESCRIPTION The sea otter is to 1.5 m (5 ft.) long and can weigh up to 45 kg (100 lb.). The thick fur is usually dark brown to black; the head, throat, and neck are far lighter in colour. The sea otter has webbed hind feet, unlike the river otter.

ETYMOLOGY The genus name *Enhydra* is Greek for "in the water."

HABITAT Coastal bays with kelp beds from Alaska to California.

CALIFORNIA SEA LION
Zalophus californianus

EARED SEAL FAMILY Otariidae

ECOLOGICAL ROLE Sea lions of the west coast are strictly carnivores. Their diet is mainly squid, mackerel, rockfish, herring, octopus, clams, and over fifty species of other fish, including salmon. Their general appearance of seeming lackadaisical is misleading. They can swim speeds up to 40 km/hr (25 mph). Sea lions' voracious appetites control the populations of many of the animals within their diet, and they themselves are an important food source to orcas.

DESCRIPTION The male California sea lion is to 2.5 m (8.2 ft.) long, and the female is to 1.7 m (5.6 ft.) long. The California sea lion is smaller than the Steller sea lion and darker in colour.

ETYMOLOGY The genus name *Zalophus* means "intense crest," from the mature male's protruding sagittal crest.

HABITAT The California sea lion is a native to the west coast of North America. It enjoys rocky and sandy beaches and will haul itself out on wharves.

PACIFIC HARBOUR SEAL

Phoca vitulina ssp. richardii

HAIR SEAL FAMILY Phocidae

ECOLOGICAL ROLE Harbour seals on the West Coast prey on salmon, squid, herring, crustaceans, molluscs, and rockfish. While they are an important food source for orcas, sharks, and sea lions, they are also vital to polar bears farther north. Though they look cute from a distance, they can weigh up to 130 kg (285 lb.) and eat over 8 kg (18 lb) of food per day.

DESCRIPTION The Pacific harbour seal is to 1.8 m (6 ft.) long. Their fur and spots vary in colour from brown to white, tan, to grey, and nearly black.

ETYMOLOGY The genus name *Phoca* means "seal." The subspecies name *richardii* commemorates Captain George Henry Richard (1820–1896), who led a British survey expedition along Vancouver Island in 1862.

HABITAT One of the most commonly seen sea mammals in the Pacific Northwest. Can be found from Alaska to California.

STELLER SEA LION
Northern Sea Lion
Eumetopias jubatus

EARED SEAL FAMILY Otariidae

ECOLOGICAL ROLE The largest of the eared seals, these enormous marine predators feed on a wide variety of species, with an average full-grown male eating more than 40 kg (88 lb.) a day. They themselves are a significant food source to orcas, while great white sharks may feed on pups.

CONSERVATION STATUS Near threatened.

DESCRIPTION Male Steller sea lions are to 3.3 m (10.7 ft.) long and can weigh up to 1,120 kg (2,470 lb.), while females are to 2.9 m (9.5 ft.) long and can weigh up to 350 kg (770 lb). Males have a broader forehead than females and a light-tan head and rust-coloured body. Females are rust-coloured all over.

ETYMOLOGY The species name *jubatus* means "one with the broad forehead," while its common name commemorates German naturalist Georg Wilhelm Steller (1709–1746), who first described them in 1741.

HABITAT Rocky coastal waters from Alaska to California.

ACKNOWLEDGEMENTS

This book could not be the quality it is without the help of many people, of whom I would like to acknowledge and thank the following: the University of British Columbia; Warren Layberry, who edited the manuscript; and the great staff at Heritage House Publishing, including editorial director Lara Kordic, editorial coordinator Nandini Thaker, and designer Rafael Chimicatti.

Having recently moved back to Vancouver Island, I wish to acknowledge that the land on which I now live and write is within the traditional territories of the Lkwungen (Esquimalt and Songhees), Malahat, Pacheedaht, Scia'new, T'Sou-ke, and W̱SÁNEĆ (Pauquachin, Tsartlip, Tsawout, Tseycum) Peoples.

PHOTO CREDITS

BIBLIOGRAPHY

Acorn, John, and Ian Sheldon. *Bugs of British Columbia*. Vancouver, BC: Lone Pine Publishing, 2001.

Bird, David M. *Birds of Western Canada*. Toronto: Dorling Kindersley, 2013.

Cannings, Richard, Tom Aversa, and Hal Opperman. *Birds of Southwestern British Columbia*. Victoria, BC: Heritage House, 2005.

Eder, Tamara, and Don Pattie. *Mammals of British Columbia*. Edmonton, AB: Lone Pine Publishing, 2001.

Harbo, Rick M. *Pacific Reef and Shore*. Madeira Park, BC: Harbour Publishing, 2006.

Lamb, Andy, and Bernard P. Hanby. *Marine Life of the Pacific Northwest*. Madeira Park, BC: Harbour Publishing, 2005.

Lederer, Roger, and Carol Burr. *Latin for Bird Lovers*. Portland: Timber Press, 2014.

Sheldon, Ian. *Seashore of British Columbia*. Edmonton, AB: Lone Pine Publishing, 1998.

Smith, Kathleen M., Nancy J. Anderson, and Katherine Beamish, eds. *Nature West Coast: A Study of Plants, Insects, Birds, Mammals and Marine Life as Seen in Lighthouse Park*. Victoria, BC: Sono Nis Press, 1988.

Varner, Collin. *Flora and Fauna of Coastal British Columbia and the Pacific Northwest* (Expanded Edition). Victoria, BC: Heritage, 2021.

INDEX

COLLIN VARNER began his career as a horticulturalist/arboriculturist at UBC in 1977, working at the Botanical Garden and, over the course of that career, assumed responsibility for conserving trees in all corners of campus, including those planted by graduating classes and ceremonial trees dating back to 1919. He retired in 2020. Varner is the author of *The Flora and Fauna of Coastal British Columbia and the Pacific Northwest* (Heritage House, 2018, 2021); *Edible and Medicinal Flora of the West Coast: British Columbia and the Pacific Northwest* (Heritage House, 2020, 2023); *Invasive Flora of the West Coast: British Columbia and the Pacific Northwest* (Heritage House, 2022); *The Flora and Fauna of Stanley Park* (Heritage House, 2022); *Gardens of Vancouver* (with Christine Allen); and a series of popular field guides, including *Plants of Vancouver and the Lower Mainland*, *Plants of the Whistler Region*, *Plants of the West Coast Trail*, and *Plants of the Gulf & San Juan Islands and Southern Vancouver Island*. He lives in Victoria, BC.